Everything You Need To Know About

YOUR
LEGAL
RIGHTS

Every individual has certain rights that can never be taken away.

Everything You Need To Know About

YOUR LEGAL RIGHTS

Kenneth Fox, Ph.D.

THE ROSEN PUBLISHING GROUP, INC.
NEW YORK

Published in 1992, 1995 by The Rosen Publishing Group, Inc.
29 East 21st Street, New York, New York 10010

Revised Edition 1995
Copyright © 1992, 1995 by The Rosen Publishing Group, Inc.

Manufactured in the United States of America.

Library of Congress Cataloging-in-Publication Data

Fox, Kenneth.
    Everything you need to know about your legal rights / Kenneth
Fox.
    (The Need to know library)
    Includes bibliographical references and index.
    Summary: Briefly discusses the legal rights of individuals,
emphasizing real-life situations in which teenagers may find
themselves.
    ISBN 0-8239-2097-6
    1. Minors—United States—Juvenile literature. 2. Civil rights—
United States—Juvenile literature. [1.Law. 2. Children's rights.
3. Civil rights.] I. Title. II. Title: Your legal rights. III. Series.
KF479.Z9F697   1992
342.73'085—dc20   91-13340
[347.30285]   CIP
                                          AC

Contents

Introduction

When the Constitution of the United States was first written, many *delegates*, people sent to represent each state, refused to sign it. They did not believe that it gave enough protection to the people. They insisted upon the addition of ten *amendments*, or changes, known as the *Bill of Rights*. The Bill of Rights is a statement of the individual *rights* held by every person in the United States. You have probably heard about some of these rights: the right to freedom of speech, religion, and the press, the right to bear arms, the right to a fair trial. Today, every person in the United States is guaranteed those rights as well as a number of others.

However, the Bill of Rights does not state *every* right a person has, nor is it always clear what each right means, to whom it applies, or how far it extends. Rights are *interpreted* by the courts, and there are limitations on them. One Supreme Court opinion states that anyone who falsely screams "Fire!" in a crowded theater threatens other theater-goers' safety because many people could be hurt or killed running out of a theater. The court decided that the right of those people to be safe was more important than the right of free speech in that situation.

Freedom of the press allows people to publish their opinions openly, without control by the government.

New Amendments Are Added

Under slavery, African-Americans in the United States were not considered full citizens and were not protected by the Bill of Rights. The Civil War was fought partly to end slavery and to give slaves the same rights as everyone else. After the war Amendment 13, abolishing slavery, was added to the Constitution. But many African-Americans and other non-white citizens were stopped from exercising their rights as citizens by racist individuals and organizations. Two more amendments were added to the Constitution, Amendment 14 (in 1868) and Amendment 15 (in 1870), guaranteeing freedom from discrimination. In the same way, in 1920, an amendment

7

was added that gave women the right to vote. More recently, the Equal Rights Amendment was proposed, guaranteeing equal rights for women, but so far it has not been *ratified*.

Recently there have been many debates about exactly what is guaranteed by the Bill of Rights. One of the most famous disputes was over flag-burning. Is burning an American flag an expression of free speech? Or is it an act of treason? The United States Supreme Court ruled that making flag-burning illegal was restricting the people's right to demonstrate and express their beliefs; it overturned a law declaring it illegal.

Another debate has been taking place over the right to bear arms. People who support gun control laws believe that this right was meant to apply only to people in a militia, a kind of army made up of citizens rather than professional soldiers. People who oppose gun control believe that this right was meant to apply to everyone who wanted to have a gun.

Everyone has heard about the debate over abortion. This too is a question of rights. Some people believe that a woman has the right to choose what happens to her body and the fetus growing inside it, and these people are backed by the Supreme Court's decision in the case of *Roe v. Wade*. Other people believe that an embryo should be considered a human being the instant it is conceived. At that moment it should gain all the rights of a person, including the right to life. They believe that abortion is murder.

The Rights of the Young

Until you are 18, the law considers you a minor. This means that laws apply differently to you. You have all your legal rights, but you are limited in how you can exercise them. For instance, you cannot be grounded without your permission when you are over 18, but when you are a minor your parents can legally restrict your movements. They can make you go to church. They can even limit what you say.

This may seem unfair; however, there are many reasons for limiting the rights of young people. Many young people are not mature enough fully to understand the responsibilities that go with the rights. For instance, no one under 18 is allowed to own a gun. This may seem like a violation of the right to bear arms, but lawmakers believed it would be too dangerous for teenagers to have guns, since they are less likely to know how to use them properly. Under the present law if you want a gun, a parent must buy it for you and make sure you understand its dangers.

Most of the limitations on the rights of the young are for your protection and safety. Some of them may seem old-fashioned and outdated. If you are having trouble with a law that seems unfair to you, you have the right to try to get that law changed, even if you are under 18.

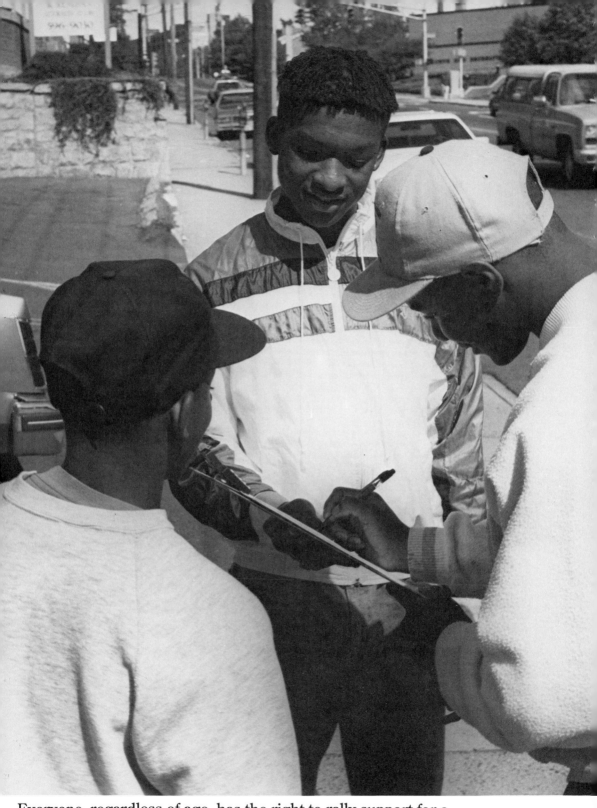

Everyone, regardless of age, has the right to rally support for a particular cause.

Chapter 1

Young People's Rights: Protection and Limits

*J*anine Givens and her friend Lee Palmer are 11 *years old. They live in Andover, Massachusetts. When they had a report to write for school, they went to the public library.*

They found only a few useful books in the children's section, so they went to the adult section. The librarian told them they had to be 12 to be allowed in the adult section. She made them go back to the children's section.

Janine's mother became upset when she heard what had happened. She tried to find out whether the girls would be allowed in the adult section if they had their parents' permission.

She found out that the library rule applied to all children under 12, whether or not they had their parents' permission. The purpose of the rule was to make sure adults were not disturbed.

Asserting Your Rights

Janine and Lee decided the library rules were keeping them from exercising an important right: the right to read. They decided to do something to get the library to change its rules.

They circulated a petition asking the library to change the rule. The petition was signed by 150 children. Local newspapers learned of the petition and printed stories about it. A large color photo of Janine and Lee holding the petition appeared in the Sunday paper.

Janine's mother and other parents said that they supported the petition also. They did not think the library had a good reason for its rule. They recognized that there were reasons for limiting young people's rights. But they did not think the library should limit their children's right to read.

Reasons for Limits on Your Rights

Everyone enjoys the same rights. Adults may exercise their rights fully. As a young person you possess the same rights, but your use of those rights can be limited for three important reasons.

• Protection

The first reason is the need for protection. Your parents have a legal responsibility to protect and care for you. In order to do this, they may limit your rights.

Your local government can also limit your rights to protect you. For example, some towns have curfews requiring young people under age 16 or 14 to be off the streets after 10:00 p.m. These curfews are meant to protect you from danger or prevent you from getting into trouble.

Some parents make many rules and punish their children for breaking these rules. They believe rules are an important way to protect their children from harm. If your parents are very strict, you may think you have no rights at all. But this is not true. Your parents can protect you by limiting your rights, but they cannot take your rights away completely.

• **Lack of Maturity**

The second reason for limiting young people's rights is their lack of maturity. Young people's powers of reasoning are not fully developed. They are often not able to separate what is good for them from what is harmful.

The PG-13 restriction on many movies states that children under 13 cannot see the movie unless accompanied by a parent or guardian. This restriction shows how limits are lifted as young people become more mature. If you are 13 or older, you are considered mature enough to see PG-13 movies without parental supervision.

Restrictions on young people's right to vote are also based on their lack of mature judgment. You cannot vote until you become 18. Until 1971, the voting age was 21. It was reduced to 18 because most people had come to believe that 18-year-olds were mature enough to vote responsibly.

• Conflict with Your Parents' Rights

The third limitation on young people's rights arises from conflict with the rights of their parents. One of the most important rights of parents is the right to decide how their children will be educated. Another is the right to determine their children's religion.

If your parents think that certain books will interfere with the way they want you to grow up, they have the right to prevent you from reading those books. In some towns, the public library keeps young people from borrowing certain books when their parents request such restriction.

You *Can* Fight City Hall

While your rights can be limited, you should never feel that your rights can be taken away.

"You can't fight city hall," people often say. They are wrong. We have the rights we have today because people throughout our history have stood up against rules and laws they believed were wrong. They fought city hall and won.

Andover's library officials are considering whether the policy should be changed. Janine and Lee are waiting to see if their petition has succeeded. If you lived in Andover, would you sign Janine and Lee's petition? Are children restricted from the adult section of the library in your community?

Chapter 2

Parental Abuse and Other Rights Violations

Many of your rights are limited by your parents. According to law, they have the right to tell you where to live, how to live, how to dress, what religion to practice, even how to choose your friends. In a way, your family is like an absolute monarchy in which your parents are king and queen and you are their subject. However, in most families, parents listen to their children before they make rules, so that the rules are more fair.

Your parents have many responsibilities that go along with their rights over you. They must never do anything that can harm you. That means that they must make sure you get a good education, have a place to live, eat well, and stay healthy physically. It also means trying to ensure that you are happy and that you have the freedom to develop and learn about

15

life. They may not abuse you mentally or physically.

Unfortunately, some parents forget or overlook these responsibilities. Thousands of children are abused in the United States when their parents do not accept these responsibilities. Children are beaten, verbally abused, neglected, even sexually abused.

If your parents do not fulfill their responsibilities, they are committing a crime. They can be arrested and jailed. If they still do not treat you properly, the courts may take you away from them. Another family would then be selected to take care of you.

Child Abuse

Kathy came to school one day with a large bruise on her arm. No one noticed until physical education class. Her teacher, seeing her arm, asked her what had happened. Her mother had hit her that morning with a wooden cutting board, Kathy said casually, acting like it didn't matter.

The PE teacher sent her to the nurse. The nurse asked Kathy how she had gotten the large bruise on her arm. Kathy told her that her mother had hit her with a wooden cutting board, but it was not big deal, her mother just gets angry sometimes. The nurse called Kathy's mother.

The nurse told Kathy's mother to take Kathy to the emergency room at the hospital. An x-ray was taken of Kathy's arm. The x-ray showed that her arm was broken. It also showed that it had been broken in the past. The doctor asked Kathy's mother when the other injury had happened. Kathy's mother said she

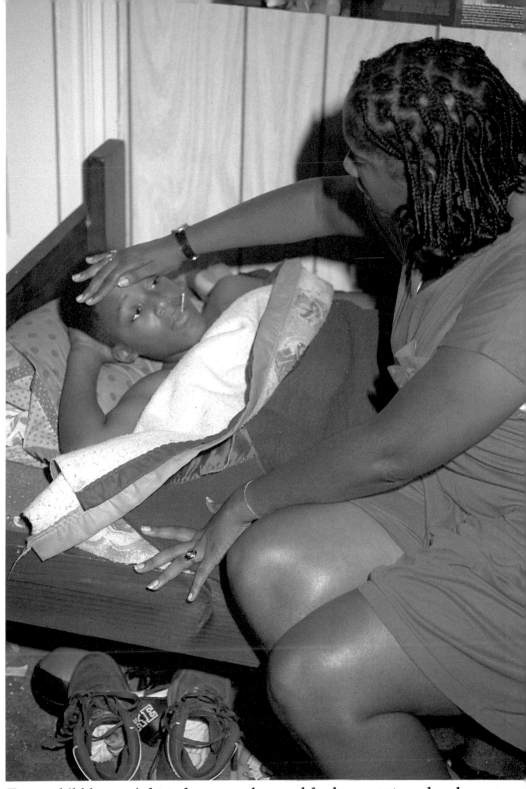

Every child has a right to be properly cared for by parents or legal guardians.

didn't know; Kathy was always bumping into things. The doctor suspected that Kathy had been abused by her parents. Parental abuse is the legal term for serious injury done to a child by the child's father or mother.

The doctor called the state Department of Child Protective Services. A caseworker arrived and spoke with Kathy. Later, Kathy's mother was arrested and taken to jail where she stayed overnight.

Kathy was scared and upset. The caseworker asked her if her mother had broken her arm. Kathy responded that she loved her mother and that she did not want anything bad to happen to her.

Many children are abused by their parents. Often the only way to protect children from abuse is to arrest the parents that hurt them.

The judge allowed Kathy's mother to return home the next day, but he ordered the family to receive counseling. Every week the family spoke with a therapist. Kathy's mother also went alone to a therapist. Discussing the problem with the therapist and the family helped. Kathy's mother learned to control her temper and to express her anger without hurting Kathy.

Child Neglect

Your parents are responsible for supporting you and taking care of your physical needs. If they do not care for you well enough, they are violating your rights. This is called *neglect*. Neglect is not always intentional. Your parents may be trying their best.

Sometimes children suffer neglect because their parents are away from home a great deal. Sometimes they cannot afford to buy food or clothing because all the money goes to pay the rent.

Parents are sometimes unaware of programs that can help them. *Medicaid* can help with medical costs, and *food stamps* can help with groceries. Some programs help pay the rent or the cost of heating in the winter.

If You Are Abused or Neglected

If your parent hits you, sexually molests you, or neglects you (failing to take care of you and leaving you to fend for yourself), you have the right to take action to protect yourself.

When you have a big problem, you probably first turn to your parents for help. But whom do you turn to when your parents are the problem?

Talk with someone you trust. Speak with a teacher or a counselor at school, a religious leader, a coach, or the sponsor of a school club whom you feel comfortable approaching. If this makes you uncomfortable, call one of the hotlines listed on page 61.

The most important thing to remember is that what is happening to you is not your fault. *No one ever deserves to be abused or neglected.* You have the right to be safe.

Divorce is the legal separation of two married people. Often, one of the parents is given custody of the children.

Chapter 3

Separation and Divorce

Separation and divorce are very traumatic events both for parents and their children. On top of the stress the situations create, all the laws that go along with them can be very confusing. It's hard to understand how a decision of your parents can affect your rights so drastically.

When married people *separate,* they agree to live in separate places. This allows them to decide whether they will get back together or choose to divorce. A *divorce* is when two people legally end their marriage. They must go to court to seek the right to divorce.

When parents separate or divorce, they or a judge must decide which parent will have custody of you. *Custody* means whom you live with, who is responsible for you, and who will make major decisions about your life. Sometimes parents are given *joint custody,* which means you live with both parents at different times, and they share responsibility. Sometimes one parent has custody, and the other has *visitation rights*. This means that the parent you live with must permit your other parent to see you. Usually the divorce or separation agreement decides how often you see your noncustodial parent.

Usually parents themselves decide who has custody. But sometimes neither parent is willing to give up custody of the child. They both want to live with their child. In this case, a judge makes the decision. The judge may ask you what you would like, or he or she may decide without asking you.

Sometimes it can be hard on you not being allowed to decide who you will live with. Many children don't have a chance to tell a judge what they want.

The Child's Best Interests

Tim knew he wanted to live with his dad after the divorce. His mom was nice and all, but his dad was great. They would go fishing together, watch ball games. Life with Dad would be great. And Mom was so much stricter. If Tim had to live with her, he knew he wouldn't have as much freedom.

When Tim's parents told him that they had decided he was to live with his mom, he was really upset. They hadn't even asked him what he wanted. Why couldn't he live with his dad? Didn't his dad love him?

His parents tried to explain to Tim that his father was out of town so often on business that it would be more stable for him to live with his mother. But Tim was furious that a decision about his life had been made for him without even asking him what he thought.

It may seem unfair that you don't get to choose where and with whom you live. But that's the law. And there is a good reason for the law. Tim might have preferred living with his father, but his father was away from home a lot. Tim would have ended up spending most of his time alone or with baby-sitters. His parents made the decision that they thought would be best for him.

If you think your parents made the wrong decision about custody, talk to them. Tell them how you feel, and listen to what they have to say. Your parents would not make such an important decision about you without thinking about it first. And remember, whatever you think, they have the right to decide where you live.

Our compulsory education laws mean that children from age 6 to 16 must go to school and must have the choice of a free education.

Chapter 4

Do I Have to Go to School?

"*I* *hate school,*" *Ramone complained as his mother shook him awake. "Why do I have to go to school? We never learn anything. All our teacher ever says is 'Be quiet! Get back in your seat!'*"

Compulsory Education

Going to school is one of your legal rights. The constitution of your state provides that you have the right to a free education. These laws are called the *compulsory education laws*. They provide that all children from age 6 to age 16 must receive an education.

Compulsory education laws were passed around 100 years ago for two reasons. The first reason was to prevent parents from forcing their children to go to work. Before, parents had the right to send their children to work instead of to school. These laws gave parents the responsibility of making sure that their children received an education.

The second reason for these laws was to make cities and towns build school buildings and hire the necessary teachers. Before the laws were passed, cities and towns often failed to raise the money to build the new schools that were needed.

Public Schools, Parochial Schools, and Private Schools

Your city or town is required to make sure there is room for you in the *public school* system. But you do not have to go to a public school. Many children attend *parochial schools* run by churches and religious groups. Other children attend *private schools* with no religious connections. Most of the money to run these schools comes from the parents of children who attend them. Cities and towns do not pay for the education of children attending parochial or private schools.

Your Rights at School

Janna and Peter wrote an article for their school newspaper about the baseball team. They charged that the four best players were not attending any of their classes. When the principal saw the article, he ordered that the papers not be given out. He removed Janna and Peter from the newspaper staff.

When Janna's mother heard what had happened, she called the principal. He told her the article could keep the baseball team from playing in the state championship game. The principal said he was trying to protect the school and the team.

Unlike most printed material, your school newspaper can be censored.

If Janna and Peter had been writing for a town newspaper, no one would have been able to interfere. However, because the paper was a school publication, the principal had the right to censor it. Because of a Supreme Court decision, a school can censor a publication if it can present a good reason for that censorship. However, if the newspaper had not been a school publication, the principal could not have prevented the papers from being distributed.

Child labor laws say that a person must be at least 16 years old in order to work legally.

Chapter 5

What If I Want to Work?

*P*erry is 13, but he is very tall for his age. He got a job at a gas station pumping gas from 3 in the afternoon until 11 at night. The station wasn't very busy in the evening. He had time between customers to work on his school assignments.

One afternoon a caseworker from the state Department of Labor came into the station. She asked the manager, Mr. Sawyer, whether Perry was old enough to be working in a gas station. He told her Perry had said he was 16.

The caseworker asked Perry whether he had a work permit. Perry said he didn't think he needed one. The caseworker said he must tell her how old he was. She was very serious. Perry knew he had to tell her his real age.

Child Labor Laws

The caseworker told the station manager he was in violation of the state's child labor law. She told Perry he would have to get a work permit. "Even with a permit," she said, "you will not be allowed to work in a gas station. The law prohibits young people under the age of 16 from working in gasoline stations and other places that are considered dangerous."

Compulsory Education and Child Labor: Two Laws that Work Together

Child labor laws were passed about 100 years ago. This was at the same time state governments passed their compulsory education laws. The two laws work hand in hand. The education laws make parents and schools see that every child is provided with an education. The child labor laws make parents and employers see that children work only when they are old enough and only under suitable conditions.

If you were working in violation of the child labor laws, you would not be penalized. Instead, your parents and the person employing you would be considered at fault.

The child labor laws also protect you from doing work that is dangerous. Perry cannot work in a gas station while he is under 16. The lawmakers in his state believed working in a gas station was dangerous for someone of that age.

There is one kind of dangerous work that young people under 16 are allowed to do: harvesting fruit and vegetables. Legislators in farm states believe that depending entirely upon adults for harvesting would cost too much money. The prices of the fruits and vegetables would be too high. Customers at the supermarket would not buy them.

Your Rights at Work

When you do work, you are protected by certain rights. You have the right to be paid for all the work you do. You have the right to be paid the *minimum wage* per hour. Minimum wages are set by Congress and by state legislatures.

You can find out what the minimum wage is in your state when you apply for a work permit. Usually work permits can be obtained at your school. If not, someone there should be able to tell you where you can get one.

Getting a work permit is important. You must have a permit to defend yourself if your rights at work are violated.

Work and School

Some young people feel that the education laws and the child labor laws *prevent* them from exercising their rights. They want to be left alone to quit school and go to work. Your rights are restricted until you are 16 for your protection. The laws protect you now and when you are 16 and older.

"Hanging out" in most public places is usually okay, unless it violates laws against loitering or creating a nuisance.

Chapter 6

On the Corner and at the Mall

*J*erome and Al live on Morris Avenue, up the hill *from their school. Tony, Ed, and Lou live down Morris Avenue in the opposite direction. After school they like to hang around on the corner before heading home. They joke about what happened that day. There may be some shoving and yelling.*

Mr. Banks owns a drug store on the same corner. Many of his customers are elderly people. They are afraid of the boys. They wish Mr. Banks would do something to stop the boys from hanging out in front of his store.

The police tell Mr. Banks that they understand his problem. They explain to him that the boys have a right to be in front of his store. The police say they can only tell the boys to move away if they are creating a nuisance.

One Person's Right Can Be Another Person's Nuisance

The legal definition of a nuisance is the same as its everyday definition: a thing or activity that interferes with someone's enjoyment, causes them physical discomfort, or makes them afraid they will be injured. These meanings are easily understood.

The problems arise when there are differences of opinion. Mr. Banks's elderly customers say the boys make them afraid. The boys insist they have a right to be on the corner. They say that they are careful not to bother Mr. Banks's customers.

Who is right? Should Mr. Banks be allowed to have the police tell the boys to move? Should the boys be allowed to continue hanging out at the corner? Also, who should decide who is right? Will the boys, Mr. Banks, and Mr. Banks's customers all have to go to court, with their lawyers, and ask a judge to decide the matter?

The best solution would be for the boys who are claiming their rights and the people who are bothered to try to come up with an answer. This might happen if the police arrested the boys and everyone went to court. Then the judge could tell everyone concerned to get together and work things out.

"Under Eighteen Not Admitted Without Parent or Guardian"

Almost everyone knows a store that refuses to let kids under age 18, or 16, enter by themselves.

Usually it is the kind of store that sells things kids like. It may sell gum, comic books, candy bars, games, records, or tapes. If you have been kept out of a store, you may have asked yourself: "Don't I have a right to go into any store I want?"

The law does recognize a person's right to shop, but it is a right that can be restricted in some ways. Owners of stores can legally prevent young people from entering. What they cannot do is allow some young people to shop but not others.

A store that allowed white kids to shop but not black or Hispanic kids would be violating the *civil rights* laws. These are laws prohibiting different treatment of people because of race, sex, physical handicap, and some other reasons. We will hear more about civil rights in Chapter 11.

Shopping Malls: Public or Private?

Shopping malls raise more complicated questions about rights. A mall is actually a very large building. Inside the building are stores similar to the stores along a street. The owners of these stores can restrict who enters. There are also open areas inside the mall. These are known as *common areas.* Legally, common areas are like city streets and sidewalks. They belong to everyone. The mall owners cannot prevent anyone from entering the mall and using these common areas.

If you have visited malls with your friends, you may have had difficulty exercising your right to walk or stand in these common areas. A mall security officer may have warned you that you will have to leave the mall if you cause trouble. You may have been told that it is illegal for more than three or four of you to stand or walk around together.

Is it legal for malls to make their own rules and force you to leave if you break a rule? Many lawyers and judges would answer "No." When the mall owners invite everyone to come into the mall, the walkways become *public property.* This means the mall owners must allow people to do all the things they have a right to do on the streets and sidewalks outside the mall.

Getting mall owners to agree not to make special rules for young people is difficult. Can you do anything about the rules at the mall you like to go to? It will not be easy. It would help to have your parents and your friends' parents request a meeting with the mall owners, the mall security officers, and the police chief and mayor or chief administrator of your town.

Such a meeting could show the mall owners that you and your friends are serious. It could show that you understand that rights come with responsibilities, and that you take your responsibilities seriously. The mall owners and security officers might be surprised to find that young people know so much about their rights.

Chapter 7

Sex and the Law

*S*ue and Chuck are in love. They sit by themselves
in the school cafeteria talking softly to each other.
After school they hide under the stands at the football
field. They hold their breath and kiss as long as they
can. Some of their friends have "gone all the way,"
but Chuck and Sue worry about having intercourse.
They don't want Sue to become pregnant.

*They also know that intercourse puts you at risk
of contracting AIDS. They had a special class in
school about sexually transmitted diseases. Neither
one of them has had sex before, so they don't think
they can give AIDS to each other. Still, they just
aren't sure. If you are worried about AIDS, you can
read about it in another book in the Need to Know
series*: Everything You Need to Know About AIDS

Your Sexual Rights

Your sexual rights are restricted until you are considered mature enough to exercise them freely. Young people mature at different ages, but states must set an official age for sexual maturity. This age is called the "age of consent." It is 18 in many states, but younger in others. Until you reach this age, it is officially "against the law" for you to have sexual intercourse.

Age of consent laws are very old-fashioned. For example, most consent laws apply only to the girl. They do not set any age of consent for the boy. This is because some consent laws were written to please fathers. Fathers wanted the legal system to punish anyone who had sex with their daughters without their permission.

The boy or man who violates the consent law is guilty of *statutory rape*. Rape occurs when a person is forced to have sex against her will. *Statutory* is a legal term. It means that a person is guilty of a crime because someone involved is younger than the age stated in a law.

A boy or man is guilty of statutory rape if the girl with whom he had sexual intercourse is younger than the age of consent. He can be found guilty and punished *even if the girl consented to having intercourse.* Until she reaches the age of consent, the law restricts a girl's right to make her own decisions about sexual matters.

People over the age of 18 have the legal right to "consent" (agree) to sex with others over that age. Everyone—no matter what their age— has the legal right to refuse sex with anyone for any reason.

Your Rights if You Become Pregnant

When Sue's friend Amanda became pregnant, she went to a family planning center to get help. The counselor at the center suggested she have a blood test to be sure she was pregnant. Amanda told the counselor she didn't know what she would do if her father found out.

Amanda's test showed she was pregnant. She asked the counselor whether she could get an abortion. An abortion removes the developing egg from a woman's uterus. This ends her pregnancy.

The counselor explained that every woman has the right to end a pregnancy through an abortion. In some states, restrictions apply to young people. Some states require that girls obtain their parents' permission before having an abortion. Other states require that the girl's parents be told, but do not require the parents' permission.

Abortions and the Law

On Sunday evening, for no apparent reason, Amanda began to cry. When Amanda got control of herself, her mother asked her what was wrong. Amanda told her about getting pregnant, and her appointment for an abortion.

Amanda's mother was very glad Amanda had told her about what had happened. She told Amanda a very deep secret. When she was 17, she had an abortion too.

"Abortions were completely illegal in those days," Amanda's mother said. *"I had it done in a doctor's office. It cost $300. My three girlfriends helped me raise the money.*

"The doctor's instruments weren't clean enough, and I got an infection," Amanda's mother said. *"My temperature went up to 105° and I almost died.*

"Since abortions were legalized," Amanda's mother reassured her, *"doctors can do them safely in hospitals or clinics. The danger of something going wrong is very small."*

The Right to Life and the Right to Choose

Up until about 20 years ago, it was illegal to have an abortion in every state in the United States. The Supreme Court gave their opinion about this. They gave their answer in a very important case called *Roe vs. Wade.*

The judges did not say that women have a right to end a pregnancy through an abortion. What they said was that ending a pregnancy is a *private* decision.

The Supreme Court judges said that government and the law cannot interfere with people's private decisions. Pregnant girls and women, along with everyone else, have a *right to privacy.* One of the things this right allows them to do is end a pregnancy by having an abortion.

Women's right to privacy also allows them to prevent pregnancy by using birth control devices. These rights are often called the *right to choose* or the *right of choice.* They refer to a woman's right to choose whether or not she wants to have a child.

Most people agree that there is such a thing as the right to privacy. Many people do not agree that pregnancy and abortion are entirely private. They believe that a baby comes to life at the moment a woman becomes pregnant. They insist that this baby has a *right to life.*

The supporters of the right to life want abortions to be made illegal again. They claim that when an abortion is performed a baby is being killed. They say abortions must become illegal to guarantee the right of these babies to live.

Your Right to Have Your Baby

Until a few years ago, a girl younger than the age of consent who became pregnant and had her baby could have the baby taken away by the legal system. Today you have the right to keep your baby in almost all cases.

You have the right to continue going to school and to bring your baby to school with you. Your school must help you take care of your baby while you attend classes. Sometimes all the mothers and their babies are together in the same classroom. The babies sleep or play while the mothers take part in classes.

Chapter 8

Drugs and Alcohol

*M*artha and Laurie were doing their homework at Laurie's house. Laurie's mother and father were at work.

"I know where my dad hides the key to the liquor cabinet," Laurie said. She got the key and opened the cabinet.

"You try this one," Laurie said, "and I'll have some of this. It smells like oranges."

"That's really sweet," Martha said. "Let's have some more of that."

"Don't have too much," Laurie said. "It makes you feel really funny."

When Martha got home she did feel funny. Her mother asked her what she did at Laurie's house.

"Were you doing something you shouldn't at Laurie's house?" her mother asked. "You look sick. Did Laurie give you liquor to drink?"

"Well, we only had a few sips," Martha said. "I didn't think it would hurt me. I guess liquor is stronger than I thought."

"Drinking can be dangerous. You have to be careful, especially at your age," her mother said.

Regulation of Alcohol

In most states, it is illegal to buy alcoholic beverages until you are 21. Until recently, some states had 18 as the *legal drinking age.* This is the same age at which young people can vote and exercise other adult rights. But with the rise of alcohol-related car accidents the age was raised to 21.

Your parents may allow you to drink at home under their supervision. Restrictions are necessary because alcohol, even in small amounts, can distort your judgment. Even for adults 21 and over, drinking is restricted. No one may drive a car if they have drunk more than a moderate amount.

Drugs: Legal and Illegal

Many drugs are regulated because they also can distort your judgment. They interfere with your ability to do ordinary tasks like driving a car.

Many drugs that doctors prescribe are dangerous. They can only be purchased at a drugstore with a prescription signed by a doctor.

You probably also know about illegal or "hard" drugs such as marijuana, cocaine, crack, and heroin. The laws against these drugs are very strict, partly because the drugs are distributed and sold by large networks of illegal suppliers and dealers that are difficult to control.

Drug traders are often involved in other illegal activities as well. Many of the people who buy and use the drugs get the money by illegal means.

Most states say you must be 21 years old to drink alcohol.

Drugs and Your Rights

Many young people are involved with drugs. Some use drugs themselves. Some sell drugs to others. You may have been offered drugs. You may know someone who uses them. Drugs are one of the biggest sources of trouble in schools today.

To fight the drug problem, many schools conduct searches of lockers and people's clothing. Many people feel that these searches violate students' rights.

The Bill of Rights protects us from *illegal searches and seizures.* This means that the police or your school principal cannot look for drugs in your pockets or your locker whenever they choose. For a search to be legal, they must have strong reasons to believe that you are concealing drugs.

You, Drugs, and Your Parents

When your parents are involved, the idea of illegal searches and seizures does not apply. Your right not to be searched does not include the right not to be searched by your parents. Their parental right to protect and care for you allows them to legally search your clothes, your room, or anything else .

It is far better for parents and children to be able to deal with these issues in an atmosphere of trust. When it comes to questions about drugs, your parents should be able to trust you to carry out the responsibilities that go along with your rights.

Chapter 9

Gerald and the Juvenile Justice System

*G*erald and his friend Ronnie called Mrs. Cook
on the telephone and said some "dirty" words to her.
Mrs. Cook called the police. The police were able to
find out that the call came from Gerald's house. They
went there and found Gerald and Ronnie. They took
them to a juvenile detention center. A juvenile detention center is a place where young people are kept
when they are arrested by the police.

The next day a juvenile court judge had a hearing
about Gerald. Juvenile courts handle cases involving
young people. They are a separate system from the
courts and judges for adults. The judge asked Gerald
questions. Mrs. Cook was not there.

A few days later there was a second hearing. The
judge decided that Gerald must go to the state industrial training school. He would have to stay there
until he reached his majority.

An industrial training school is not a regular school. It is actually a type of jail for young people. Majority is the age at which a person legally becomes an adult. In most states an 18-year-old is considered an adult. Gerald was 15.

Gerald's parents spent three years going to other courts trying to get Gerald free. Finally, the Supreme Court decided that Gerald's parents were right. By that time, Gerald had become 18.

If you believe any of your legal rights have been violated, you can seek the advice of a lawyer.

Gerald and the Supreme Court

What happened to Gerald is a true story. Gerald's full name is Gerald Gault.

The Supreme Court said that Gerald was prevented from exercising his rights. A person who is arrested has several rights.

• The right to be considered innocent until proved otherwise.

• The right to be represented by a lawyer.

• If the arrested person cannot pay a lawyer, the government must provide one.

• The right to refuse to answer any questions that may *incriminate*—make the person seem guilty.

• The right to see the people who say you broke the law and to ask them any questions.

Since Gerald won his case, things have changed a great deal. If you are arrested today and brought before a judge, you have the right to be represented by a lawyer. The police and the judge must prove that you did the things you are accused of doing. They must let your lawyer try to prove that you did *not* do what the police claim you did.

You can *appeal* the decision of the judge. In an appeal, you ask a second judge to determine whether mistakes were made at your trial and whether your rights were restricted or denied.

The law provides citizens with many rights if they are arrested or
taken into custody.

Chapter 10

The Juvenile Justice System and You

There are two ways in which you can become involved with the juvenile justice system. The first is to be *taken into custody* for breaking the law. Being taken into custody means that a police officer or court officer takes you to a juvenile detention center. There they indicate what crime you have been accused of.

Being taken into custody is like being arrested. The difference is that you can be taken without proof if a police officer or court officer *thinks* you have done something wrong.

In many cases, if the young people who were taken into custody had been treated the way adults are treated, they could not have been arrested. Why not? Because there was not enough evidence to prove they had committed crimes.

You can also be brought into the juvenile justice
system if you cannot control how you act and your
parents are no longer able to help you control yourself. In some states you would be referred to as a
Person In Need of Supervision (PINS for short).

The most common reasons young people are
considered in need of supervision are (1) being
repeatedly absent from school, (2) running away
from home, and (3) constantly fighting with their
parents. You do not have to break a specific law or
commit a crime to become a PINS.

How the Juvenile Justice System May Treat You

If you are taken into the system, you have the
right to *due process*. Due process is a legal term
meaning that all of your rights must be respected.
These include your right to be represented by a
lawyer and your right to know the exact reasons
why you have been brought in. These rights are
discussed in Chapter 9.

If a judge decides something must be done
about you, there are three kinds of action she or he
can order. The first is *probation*. Probation is a
legal term meaning that you will be supervised by
an officer of the court for a specific period of time.
The officers are called *probation officers*. The period of time might be as short as six months or as
long as two or three years.

If you are on probation you must meet regularly with a probation officer. Usually you will agree to certain things that the officer thinks are necessary.

The second type of action the judge might order is that you attend a special school. Sometimes these are called industrial training schools, the type Gerald Gault was sent to in Arizona. Sometimes they are called *reform schools*. These schools are basically prisons, but they do provide courses like ordinary schools. The doors are locked, however, and the outdoor areas are fenced in.

Being Tried as an Adult

The third type of action the judge can order is that you be tried as an adult. When this happens, your case is transferred to a regular judge of the criminal court system. You may have a trial, or you may arrange a *plea bargain*. In a plea bargain, the person charged with committing a crime agrees to admit being guilty. The judge responds by ordering a less severe punishment.

The number of young people tried as adults has been increasing steadily. Most of these young people have committed very serious crimes. For example, if a young person kills someone with a gun, he or she will probably be tried as an adult. A young person who is heavily involved in drug dealing can also be tried by the courts as an adult.

If someone is tried as a juvenile, the judge cannot order a sentence that continues beyond age 21.

Rosa Parks helped to spark the civil rights movement of the 1960s. In Alabama in 1955, she refused to give up her seat on a bus to a white person.

Chapter 11

Things *Can* Change

January 15 is the day Americans honor Dr. Martin Luther King, Jr. for his accomplishments as a leader of the *civil rights movement* in the United States. The civil rights movement was a struggle to make sure that all people can fully exercise their rights. Age, sex, race, or religion cannot be the reason for treating any one person differently from another.

The struggle for American civil rights began in colonial times. On July 4, Americans celebrate the adoption of the Declaration of Independence in 1776. The Declaration was another important part of the struggle for our rights. On Presidents' Day, in February, Americans honor George Washington and Abraham Lincoln. As the first president of the United States, Washington helped make sure that the Bill of Rights was added to the Constitution.

Abraham Lincoln was president of the United
States during the Civil War. We remember him for
helping to eliminate slavery. After the Civil War,
important amendments were added to the Constitution. These amendments made slavery illegal, gave
ex-slaves the right to vote, and guaranteed all U.S.
citizens equal protection under the law.

First Blacks, Then Women, Then Young People

Women have also been prevented from exercising their rights fully and equally. In the United
States, the struggle for women to exercise their
right to vote went on for almost a hundred years.
Finally an amendment to the Constitution was
passed guaranteeing that no one could prevent
women from voting.

Soon after 1963, women began to realize that
their rights were limited in many of the ways black
people's rights were restricted. A new women's
rights movement began.

An important part of the movement for young
people's rights began with what happened to Gerald
Gault. Gerald and his parents fought to get him the
same rights adults have when they are arrested.

Another part of the movement involved freedom
of speech. John Tinker, Mary Beth Tinker, and
Christopher Eckhardt were high school students in
Des Moines, Iowa. They wore black armbands to
school to protest against the war in Vietnam.

After being shot in an assassination attempt in 1981, James Brady worked to strengthen laws against guns. In 1991, a gun-control measure—known as the Brady Bill— was finally approved by Congress.

Their principal suspended them from school until they gave up wearing the armbands. Like Gerald Gault, they appealed in the courts and finally reached the Supreme Court.

The Supreme Court said that their right to freedom of speech gave them the right to wear the armbands to school. As long as what they were doing did not interfere with classes, the principal could not suspend them.

Experts in legal rights often say that young people did not begin to be treated as people until the Supreme Court decided these two cases: the case of Gerald Gault and the case of the Tinkers and their friend. The Supreme Court said that young people have the same rights as adults. It said young people's exercise of their rights could be restricted. But they could not be treated as if they had no rights at all.

Back to the Beginnings and on to the Future

This brings us back to the question we discussed in the Introduction. What do your rights have to do with being right?

The answer is that your rights make it possible for you to do what you think is right. If someone tells you what you are doing is wrong, ask them to give you reasons. If you have to "fight city hall," or your school principal, get other kids to help you. Ask your parents to help you too.

Remember that rights come with responsibilities attached. You must show that you can act responsibly, you must respect other people's rights.

Remember also that our laws are always changing. As young people have shown that they can exercise their rights responsibly, the laws have been changed to allow them more freedom. You can keep this progress going. Other young people did it before you. Now it is your turn.

Glossary—*Explaining New Words*

abortion A procedure that removes a developing ovum or "egg," ending a pregnancy.

abuse Treating someone in a way that is cruel and harmful.

age of consent Age at which young people may marry without parental permission; also age at which a young woman may legally agree to have sexual intercourse.

appeal A procedure that allows a young person to take the decision of a juvenile court judge to another, higher court.

Bill of Rights The proclamation of your most important rights and freedoms in the first ten amendments to the Constitution.

civil rights The personal rights and freedoms of individuals.

custody An official decision, by a judge, about who will be responsible for taking care of a child or a young person.

divorce The legal ending of a marriage.

freedom of speech Your right to say what you wish whenever and wherever you desire.

freedom of the press Your right to print whatever you wish in a book, pamphlet, newspaper, or magazine.

industrial training school A special school that supervises young people who have committed serious crimes.

juvenile court   A system of judges and officers who listen to complaints against young people.

juvenile detention center   Where young people are kept before they see a juvenile court judge.

lawyer   A person who legally practices law.

minimum wage   The lowest amount of money per hour that may be paid legally to a worker.

neglect   A failure to do the things one is required to do for another person.

nuisance   A thing or activity that interferes with someone's enjoyment, causes them physical discomfort, or makes them afraid they will be injured.

PINS   Person In Need of Supervision; a young person who cannot be controlled by his or her parents or teachers.

rape   Forcing a woman to have sexual intercourse against her will.

reform school   A school that supervises young people who have committed serious crimes.

rehabilitation   Enabling people to learn to control their behavior.

rights   Your basic freedom.

separation   A legal agreement between husband and wife to live apart.

Supreme Court   The highest court in the American legal system, made up of nine judges appointed by the President.

work permit   A document that allows a young person to work at a particular job.

Where to Get Help

If going to your parents is a problem, go to teachers you trust, your friends' parents, your school librarian, school nurse, or a minister, rabbi, or YWCA or YMCA leader you know and trust.

Local and State Agencies: Public Defender's Office, Legal Aid Society, Legal Assistance Association, state chapter or affiliate of the American Civil Liberties Union.

National Organizations:

American Civil Liberties
    Union
Children's Rights Project
132 West 43rd St.
New York, NY 10036
(212) 944-9800

Youth Law Center
114 Sansome St.
San Francisco, CA 94104
(415) 543-3379

Children's Defense Fund
    Legal Division
25 East St., NW
Washington, DC 2001
(202) 628-8787

NAACP Legal Defense
    Fund
99 Hudson St. 16th Fl.
New York, NY 10013
(212) 219-1900

Child Abuse Prevention Information Resources Center
    1 (800) 342-7472
Decade of the Child Information Line
(Programs serving families & children)
    1 (800) 345-5437
Youth Crisis & Runaway Hotline (24 hrs)
    1 (800) 448-4663

For Further Reading

Atkinson, Linda. *Your Legal Rights.* New York, NY: Franklin Watts, 1982.

Berry, Joy. *Every Kid's Guide to the Juvenile Justice System.* Chicago, IL: Children's Press, 1987.

Guggenheim, Martin, and Alan Sussman. *The Rights of Young People.* An American Civil Liberties Handbook. New York, NY: Bantam Books, 1985.

Olney, Ross, and Patricia Olney. *Up Against the Law: Your Rights as a Minor.* New York, NY: Lodestar Books, 1986.

Price, Janet, and Alan Levine and Eve Cary. *The Rights of Students.* An American Civil Liberties Handbook. Southern Illinois University Press, 1988.

Sloan, Irving. *Youth and the Law.* Dobbs Ferry, NY: Oceana, 1981.

Index

About the Author

Kenneth Fox is an author and a university professor. He was co-director of the Washington Mini-School in Washington, D.C., an experimental program for sixth graders about government, the law, young people's rights, and making places for children in adult organizations. He has written on the law and American cities an on the history of American cities. He has taught history and public administration at the University of Massachusetts, Yale University, and Rutgers University.

Acknowledgments and Photo Credits

Cover photo by Chuck Peterson.
All other photographs by Stuart Rabinowitz, except page 2, Chris Volpe; page 50,©Jean Marc Giboux/Gamma Liaison; page 54,57, Wide World Photos

Design: Blackbirch Graphics, Inc.
Font: Century Old Style